He Chose Me:

Discovering Sonship Through Adoption

Kevin X. Strange

He Chose Me: Discovering Sonship Through Adoption

Published by Burning Bush Books

Copyright © by Kevin X. Strange

All rights reserved

No part of this publication may be reproduced, stored in any retrieval system, or be transmitted in any form, or by any means, mechanical, electronic, photocopying or otherwise without the prior written consent of the publisher, except as provided by United States of America copyright law.

First edition June 2020

For bulk purchases, please contact Adrienne Mayfield, Burning Bush Books, at

amayfield2147@gmail.com.

Manufactured in the United States of America

ISBN: 978-0-9997694-6-1

All Scripture quotations, unless otherwise noted, taken from the Holy Bible, New King James Version.

Cover Design: Holy Spirit, Kevin Strange, and Desy Suryani

Visit the author's website at kevinxstrange.com

Dedication

I am very excited about this book. It is a key to having a life submitted to God. I dedicate this book to all believers and followers of Jesus who have never been told there is more to Christianity than salvation. It is also dedicated to those who have not yet accepted Christ as their Savior. I pray this book will reach the hands of those who are seeking a deeper revelation of God. One encounter with Him transforms us from the inside.

Jesus didn't come to condemn the world but to redeem it. Through that redemption, He opened the door to joy, happiness on the earth, and so much more than life after death.

Table of Contents

Foreword 1

Chapter One The Big Picture: Creation 5

Chapter Two We Are at War 11

Chapter Three Salvation 19

Chapter Four Adoption – Our Identity in Christ 25

Chapter Five Our Relationship with Christ 29

Chapter Six Walking in Your Authority 33

Chapter Seven He Chose Me 37

Conclusion 39

Foreword

I am very happy you are reading this book, but I must admit that when Holy Spirit told me I was going to write another book, I thought He was joking. As you can see, He was not. It wasn't until after I completed my first book, *Breaking Point – A Revelation of the Father's Love* that I discovered the personal impact of my writing. Telling my story helped me recover from the bondage of rejection, perversion, and disappointment that had been a big part of my life and identity. Now, I am continuing that process by sharing additional revelation I have received since publication. First, I will give you a quick review of *Breaking Point* to illustrate the power of partnering with Holy Spirit to become all God intended for us.

I was born in a small town in northeast Georgia where I was raised by my mother and stepfather. My biological parents divorced while my mother was pregnant with me. As a result of their separation and my mom's trauma, the spirit of rejection entered my life while I was growing in her womb. Unborn children are not only affected by the food their mothers eat; babies also feel their mother's emotions. My mother lived with the trauma of shame and fear everyday as she tried to move forward in life. Meanwhile, I was growing inside her. Unfortunately, her shame led to a self-hatred that birthed rejection in me. That rejection led to my belief that I was gay.

Today, being gay does not come with the level of alienation it carried in 1968. Not only was it shunned in society, but there was also even more stigma attached to being gay in the church. Because my family was Baptist and deeply religious, I could never be honest about who I really was. As a matter of fact, being gay was a secret I would wrestle with for much of my teenage and early adult life.

As I grew up, I did what most every other gay person at the time did; I tried to hide it and become what was expected of me. I never really dated girls, but I did have enough interest in them to get prom dates. As time moved on, I graduated from high school and moved away to attend college in Atlanta, GA. At that time, Atlanta was a thriving metropolis with an open and progressing homosexual community. The community of acceptance allowed me to finally be myself and come out as a gay man.

Coming out was very liberating. Being with more gay people gave me freedom. Gay couples were slowly gaining representation on TV and in the movies. I finally felt like I belonged. I became hopeful that maybe my life was not going to be full of heartbreak and loneliness. Still, one question remained. What was I going to do about my family? More importantly, what was I going to do about my relationship with God? Even though I was becoming more comfortable in my own skin, I couldn't help wondering how God felt about my lifestyle. Would He send me to hell for acting on feelings I believed He gave me? Or accept my feelings?

This was all too much to really think about, so I just pushed it to the back of my mind and listened to the people around me. From them, I received a daily dose of encouragement, "It's your life. Be happy and love whoever you want." Their support solidified my belief that there was nothing wrong with my choice to live as a homosexual man.

Let's fast forward to 2009. I was living my best life. I had a great job, a big house, expensive cars, and lots of friends. I had everything going for me based on the world's standard. All my "success" set the stage for a much-needed encounter with Jesus that changed my life forever. He revealed that God, Yahweh, created me for a purpose that I was aborting. He showed me God had another plan for my life. At the time of the encounter, God revealed there was more to my existence than acquiring things the world said were important. He had created me for more!

To walk in my purpose, I needed to be transformed into the person God created. I would have to embrace my true identity as a heterosexual man. After the encounter, I no longer believed I was created gay. This shift in thinking was a huge departure from the beliefs I had always held. Prior to this encounter, everything about my identity was attached to my belief that I was born homosexual. I had focused a great deal of energy on proving that being gay and black in the South didn't stop me from achieving the American Dream—money, houses, cars—all the finer things in life.

Before 2009, Jesus was nowhere on our radars. No one in my circle made Yeshua, Jesus, a focus. Although I had been raised in the church, I only went there at Christmas and Easter to visit my family.

All that changed in February of 2009. I accepted Jesus as my Saviour and started reading the Bible for myself. I joined a local Baptist church that had a solid foundation of Scripture. I learned more about God and Jesus, as well as

Foreword

what it means to be a disciple of Jesus Christ. I assumed that since my salvation gave me freedom from eternal damnation in hell, things would change for me and life would be *fantastic* until I went on to heaven. That was a fallacy. Nothing could be further from the truth. Life didn't just automatically turn into a utopia because I had chosen to make Jesus Lord of my life.

I still struggled with a mind that had been programmed by society and homosexuality. I needed additional power to undo the programming, so I could serve God instead of Satan. I soon discovered God had provided that power by sending the Holy Spirit to live inside me. Although I had heard about Holy Spirit, I did not know who He really was. Reference to Him was always made as though He was an "it," some inanimate force, not a person. I had not been introduced to Him as part of the Godhead who came to help me look and think like Jesus.

I am excited to share with you what I have learned about Holy Spirit. Learning how to build a relationship with Him will ultimately help you build an amazing relationship with Jesus, which in turn teaches you how to access the Father. Living an abundant life is all about cultivating relationships with each one of them. I can now call out to our heavenly Father in times of trouble. He picks me up, sits me on His lap and asks, "What is it my son? What is troubling you? Remember, I will never leave you. I will be with you for all eternity. You do not have to carry these burdens alone. You are my son, and I love you." He says to you today, as he says to me, "Always remember that no matter what happens, 'I Chose You.'"

Chapter One

The Big Picture: Creation

We are not products of the popular theory of evolution. We are created by God with spirits, souls, and bodies. Our multi-faceted nature plays a key role in our lives and lends clarity to the struggles we encounter.

The **spirit** is where we find what we call our intellect, emotions, passions, and creativity. The **soul** makes up our mental abilities as living beings. It is where our character, feelings, memories, and thinking take place. The **body** is the container designed to house the spirit and soul in the physical world. We need a body because both the spirit and soul were created by God to live forever. They cannot be destroyed once created. On the other hand, the body was only designed to exist temporarily on the earth. You may not have realized this, but God created the spirit and soul with eternity in mind because you are very valuable to Him. *"He has made everything beautiful in its time. He has also set eternity in the hearts of humans; yet they cannot fathom what God has done from beginning to end"* Ecclesiastes 3:11. This proves that

The Big Picture: Creation

God had plans for you from the very beginning.

You may have never heard this before, but every life (soul/spirit) that is born is a divine creation of God made for a specific purpose. *"Everyone who is called by My name, whom I have created for My glory; I have formed him, yes, I have made him"* Isaiah 43:7. *"For in him all things were created: things in heaven and on earth, visible and invisible, whether thrones or powers or rulers or authorities; all things have been created through him and for him"* (Colossians 1:16. These Scriptures alert us to the fact that God has a purpose for each life. We were created to bring glory to God for all eternity.

Now that we understand the reason for human life and how important it is to God, let us turn to the Scriptures to better understand the big picture from the beginning. In Genesis 1:26-27, we see the creation of the first life:

Then God said, "Let Us make man in Our image, according to Our likeness; let them have dominion over the fish of the sea, over the birds of the air, and over the cattle, over all the earth and over every creeping thing that creeps on the earth." So, God created man in His own image; in the image of God He created him; male and female He created them.

After Adam was created, God made a body to house his spirit and soul as depicted in Genesis 2:7, *"And the Lord God formed man of the dust of the ground, and breathed into his nostrils the breath of life; and man became a living being."* God created a beautiful garden called Eden for Adam and placed him there to rule. God gave him one warning, *"Of every tree of the garden you may freely eat; but of the tree of the knowledge of good and evil you shall not eat, for in the day that you eat of it you shall surely die"* Genesis 2:17. The prerequisites for Adam to have eternal life were clear. He could not eat of the tree of the knowledge of good and evil. After creating Adam and revealing His expectations, God created Eve.

The Lord God said, "It is not good that man should be alone; I will make him a helper comparable to him... And the Lord God caused a deep sleep to fall on Adam, and he slept; and He took one of his ribs and closed up the flesh in its place. Then the rib which the Lord God had taken from man He made into a woman, and He brought her to the man. Genesis 2:18, 21-22

Things were off to a great start for humanity. Adam and Eve were given instructions, and they had the ability to commune with God on a regular basis. God walked and talked with them just as any loving Father would. He provided their every need as He was their sole provider. Eventually, they procreated and filled the earth with other humans who would carry the legacy of God for all eternity.

God created man and animals, as well as other beings—angels. God, Jesus, and Holy Spirit live in heaven where angels also dwell. Angels are supernatural beings, but they have something in common with humans—as created beings they are also subject to God.

One particular angel played an important role in the book of Genesis, a fallen angel named Lucifer. In Ezekiel 28:11-14, we learn,

*You were the seal of perfection, full of wisdom and perfect in beauty. You were in Eden, the garden of God; every precious stone adorned you: carnelian, chrysolite and emerald, topaz, onyx and jasper, lapis lazuli, turquoise and beryl. Your settings and mountings were made of gold; on the day you were **created** they were prepared. You were anointed as* *a guardian cherub, for so **I** <u>ordained you</u>. You were on the holy mount of God; you walked among the fiery stones.*

As we can see, God went to great lengths to design a creature of brilliance. He adorned him with beautiful jewels and gave him an extremely high position of authority. However, despite his position, Lucifer was not satisfied. He wanted more. In Ezekiel 28:18-19, we learn,

*You were blameless in your ways from the day you were created **till wickedness was found in you**. Through your widespread trade you were filled with violence, and you <u>**sinned**</u>. So, I drove you in disgrace from the mount of God, and I expelled you, guardian cherub, from among the fiery stones. Your heart became proud on account of your beauty, and you corrupted your wisdom because of your splendor. So, **I** threw you to the <u>earth</u>; **I** made a spectacle of you before kings. By your many **<u>sins</u>** and dishonest trade, you have desecrated your sanctuaries. So, **I** made a <u>fire come out from you, and it consumed you</u>, and I reduced you to ashes on the ground in the sight of all who were watching. All the nations who knew you are appalled at you; you have come to a horrible end and will be no more.*

Wow, right? Not the best ending for a being created with such adornments and high position in God's kingdom. Nevertheless, we see that rebellion against God would not be tolerated. Before we move on, I want to reiterate a few key points we have covered so far.

Mankind

1. We are created in the image of God, Jesus, and Holy Spirit.
2. We are three-part beings. We are spirits who have

souls who live in bodies. The spirit and soul are eternal, but the body returns to the dirt from which we were formed.
3. We were given dominion over the Earth and instructed to replenish and manage it.
4. God promised to provide for our *every need* and give us eternal life.
5. Adam and Eve were given one rule. They could not eat from the tree of the knowledge of good and evil.

Lucifer (Satan)

Lucifer was and is a created being. He is a fallen angel who had a very high standing in heaven. Unlike humans, he was not created in the image of God.

1. Although he is powerful, he is still a created being. Hence, he is subject to the power and will of God, Jesus, and Holy Spirit.
2. Because of his great beauty and splendor, his heart became full of pride. He devised a scheme to overthrow God and convinced 1/3 of the angels in heaven to join him. Wickedness was found in him, so he was banished as a guardian angel. God cast him and his followers down to the earth.
3. After being cast down to the earth, Lucifer was known as Satan and his angelic followers were called fallen angels or demons. Their new plan was to roam the earth trying to convince all humans to rebel against God. If they succeeded, these humans would suffer the same fate as the Satan and fallen angels—eternity in Hell.

Chapter Two

We Are at War

God created many things, but His greatest creation is mankind. We are the only creation made in the likeness of God the Father, God the Son, and God the Holy Spirit.

Then God said, Let Us make man in Our image, according to Our likeness; let them have dominion over the fish of the sea, over the birds of the air, and over the cattle, over all the earth and over every creeping thing that creeps on the earth. Genesis 1:26

God spent a lot of time with Adam and Eve. They literally had the best of both worlds. They communicated with Him, yet had dominion over the place where they lived. Most importantly, they enjoyed unbroken fellowship with the Father.

It is key to remember that Satan was also on the earth at the time. He was seething over his fallen state and angered by God's love for Adam and Eve. Adam and Eve occupied a position that likely caused Satan much consternation. I can only imagine some of the thoughts that went through his mind. "They are not as beautiful as I am. They don't have knowledge as I do. They are covered in flesh made from dirt, and I am made of precious stones and gems. They are confined to this place, but I have traveled among the stars. Yet, He adores them!" Day by day, his hatred rose. He had to devise a plan of rebellion. How could he get these humans to rebel against God? Finally, he came up with a strategy. He decided to challenge their idea of God and their relationship with Him. He used the same strategy he uses today. He convinced them to question their identity.

He likely concluded, "If I can convince them to sin against God by disobeying His commandments, God, being a righteous judge will have no choice but to judge them and cast them into the pit of hell along with me and my demons. I will win over Him. *"He shall call to the heavens from above, And to the earth, that He may judge His people: Gather My saints together to Me, Those who have made a covenant with Me by sacrifice. Let the heavens declare His righteousness, For God Himself is Judge. Selah"* Psalm 50:4-6.

Satan was cast down to the earth so he could observe Adam and Eve to determine his plan of attack. Satan is not our friend. He is the enemy of God, and he hates us. His primary goal is to separate us from God and coerce us into spending eternity in Hell with him. We are warned, *"Be sober, be vigilant; because your adversary the devil walks about like a roaring lion, seeking whom he may devour"* 1 Peter 5:8. Satan is constantly working to devour us. In fact, Jesus told us that Satan's objective is three-fold: to steal, kill, and destroy. John 10:10.

Perhaps you wonder why Satan didn't just kill Adam

and Eve. We must go back to the beginning to get an adequate understanding of this diabolical plan. Satan isn't just after our bodies. He wants our souls. Our souls make the decision to obey or reject God's plan. Killing the body is not enough. He wants to collect souls. We must never forget that Satan is playing for keeps.

His plan was to get Adam and Eve to forget their identity. He enticed them to forget that they were made in the image of God. He reasoned that convincing them to question their identity and the purity of God's intention toward them would cause them to sin against God. Their disobedience would mandate that God punish them.

One day, Satan put his plan into action. He focused on the instruction God gave Adam and Eve. Remember that in Chapter 1 God told Adam and Eve exactly what they should and shouldn't eat. There was a particular tree in the garden they were not to eat from. God was clear. *"But of the tree of the knowledge of good and evil you shall not eat, for in the day that you eat of it you shall **surely die**"* Genesis 2:17.

Day in and day out, Adam and Eve tended the garden. They ate fruits and vegetables approved by God. They walked and talked with God throughout the day and built a loving relationship with their Father.

Satan, their adversary, was ready to put his plan into action. He approached Eve while she was in the garden, and engaged her in dialogue.

Has God indeed said, 'You shall not eat of every tree of the garden'? And the woman said to the serpent, "We may eat the fruit of the trees of the garden, but of the fruit of the tree which is in the midst of the garden, God has said, 'You shall not eat it, nor shall you touch it, lest you die. Genesis

3:1-3

Satan used Eve's awareness to lay a trap for her. This is the exact strategy he uses today. He is well aware that God will not betray His character for anyone or anything. He knows that sinning against God will cost us our position with Him and ultimately our eternal souls.

He confirmed Eve's awareness of the consequences and proceeded with his plan. He created doubt in her mind about God's credibility and His intentions for her:

*You will **not surely** die. For God knows that in the day you eat of it your eyes will be opened, and **you will be like God**, knowing good and evil. So, when the woman saw that the tree was good for food, that it was pleasant to the eyes, and a tree desirable to make one wise, she took of its fruit and ate. She also gave to her husband with her, and he ate.* Genesis 3:4-6

With the insertion of one word, Satan piqued Eve's interest. Was God really holding out on them? Was He withholding the tree because He knew the fruit would make them like Him? Satan managed to draw them into conversation, question the identity they were created with and strip them of their perfect lives forever. Unfortunately, they chose to take the bait. Eve ate the fruit and shared it with Adam.

Then the eyes of both of them were opened, and they knew that they were naked; and they sewed fig leaves together and made themselves coverings. And they heard the sound of the LORD God walking in the garden in the cool of the day, and Adam and his wife hid themselves from the presence of the LORD God among the trees of the garden. Then the LORD God called to Adam and said to him, "Where are you?" So, he said, "I heard Your voice in the garden, and I was afraid because I was naked; and I hid myself." Genesis 3:7-10

Just like that, the spirit of fear and shame entered the earth. Adam and Eve disobeyed the commandment of God. Immediately, they realized they were naked and viewed it as being wrong. Worse still, they feared the very Father who created them and attempted to hide from His presence. One minute they were walking and talking with God; now, their fellowship was broken.

God appeared and began searching for them. He questioned where they were. Of course, He already knew, but He did so to reveal their fallen state to them. He posed the following questions:

And He said, "Who told you that you were naked? Have you eaten from the tree of which I commanded you that you should not eat? Then the man said, "The woman whom You gave to be with me, she gave me of the tree, and I ate. And the LORD God said to the woman, "What is this you have done?" The woman said, "The serpent deceived me, and I ate. Genesis 3:11

This scenario is no different from humans today. God provides us with specific instructions on what is acceptable to Him, but we listen to the wrong voices and find ourselves in bad situations. Often, we suffer consequences beyond our ability to repair. But I am here to tell you, God has a plan to help us today. His name is Jesus. But I don't want to jump ahead too far.

Because of His holiness, God was left with no choice but to divvy out consequences. God cursed Satan and made him crawl around on his belly for the remainder of his days. He also put enmity between him and all humans coming after them. To Eve, He said, *"I will greatly multiply your sorrow and your conception; In pain you shall bring forth children; Your desire shall be for your husband, and he shall rule over you."* Genesis 3:16. To Adam, God said,

> *Because you have heeded the voice of your wife, and have eaten from the tree of which I commanded you, saying, 'You shall not eat of it': "Cursed is the ground for your sake; in toil you shall eat of it all the days of your life. Both thorns and thistles it shall bring forth for you, and you shall eat the herb of the field. In the sweat of your face you shall eat bread till you return to the ground, for out of it you were taken; for dust you are, and to dust you shall return.* Genesis 3:17

God was forced to exile Adam and Eve. *"So, He drove out the man; and He placed cherubim at the east of the garden of Eden, and a flaming sword which turned every way, to guard the way to the tree of life"* Genesis 3:24. I can only imagine the heartbreak God felt at that moment. He knew humans were not built to handle evil; yet, they chose to disobey Him and fell for the lie. That mistake started a disastrous course for Adam and Eve, as well as all their descendants, until a way out was created through Jesus.

Satan destroyed the perfect family through deception and cunning words. He exposed the human race to unimaginable evil. Eve did not sin alone. Her husband Adam was equally as guilty for not stepping in and resisting Satan. Their inability to obey God's commandment introduced sin into the world, guaranteeing that we were all born with sinful natures.

You have just read about temptation, which begins with a simple desire that stirs inside you. It could be hunger, curiosity, or being enticed. In Adam and Eve's case, I believe it was a little of each. *"So, when the woman saw that the tree was good for food, that it was pleasant to the eyes, and a tree desirable to make one wise, she took of its fruit and ate. She also gave to her husband with her, and he ate"* Genesis 3:6. This was an open door for Satan. He saw his opportunity to strike. He knew the fruit of the tree of knowledge of good and evil looked delicious. When Satan suggested they eat it, he knew their disobedience would cost them dearly. God gave this couple commandments, but He also gave them the ability to choose. Satan encouraged them to use their "free will" to disobey God.

You may be asking yourself, "What does this have to do with me? I am not trying to raise a revolt against God. I am just trying to live my best life. I am doing my own thing based on how I feel." This has everything to do with you because we are descendants of the first two humans God ever created. Therefore, we are bound by the same judgments and consequences of sin. God gives us the opportunity to choose disobedience or obedience, darkness or light, God or Satan.

Let's recap how easily these events occurred to demonstrate how simply it happens today. All three parts of Adam and Eve's personhood were involved.

The **soul** got tripped up by applying intellect to the conversation, "not surely." By inserting these two words, Eve's mind began to process the information. She likely reasoned, "God loves us. He comes down every day to talk and walk in the garden with us. He couldn't really mean that we will die."

The **body** got tripped with the eyes by looking at the fruit. Sight gave way to the engagement of the brain which, in turn, stimulated the taste buds and appetite. They all agreed that the fruit looked good for eating and would most likely be very tasty. Therefore, they concluded the fruit should be eaten.

The **spirit** was fighting an uphill battle since it was two against one. The war that Satan started with God in Heaven is now humanity's war. If we do not reconcile with God, we will suffer the same fate as Satan and his demon—a life in Hell, separated from God for all eternity. Satan managed to use his cunning nature and smooth tongue to get the first humans to sin against God and he entices us to do the same. The only hope we have is to reconnect our spirit to the Father so we can transform our sinful nature into one that pleases Him.

Chapter Three

Salvation

The previous chapter may have left you thinking or feeling all is lost. How are we supposed to fight against such a cunning adversary? There's good news! We don't have to do it alone. If we attempt to, we will lose. God has a better plan. Through a relationship with Jesus, we can be born again and be reconciled with God.

Satan thought his plan would condemn mankind and levy an eternal blow to God's creation, but God declared, "not so!" Remember that Satan is a created being. Though he is extremely cunning, he is not God. God alone is God and has a plan for everything. He is never surprised or caught off guard because He is omnipotent: all-powerful, omniscient: all-knowing, and omnipresent: everywhere at the same time, past, present, and future.

Satan's stealth is no match for God. Even as Satan was carrying out his plan of deception, God had already created a plan of redemption—one that would allow humanity a choice between good and evil. A perfect plan that, when chosen, allows us to opt for the goodness of a loving Father and eternity in Heaven or death and torment for eternity with Satan and his demons in Hell.

God, in His mercy, didn't want to leave humanity in this predicament. He knew the only way to redeem us was to send a sinless Savior to take on the sins of the world. Jesus laid down His deity to become a baby born by a virgin. He walked on the earth and lived a sinless life. Then He died a horrific death on a cross to take on the sins of the world. After three days in the grave, Holy Spirit revived Him. He conquered death and purchased the forgiveness of sins for all humanity.

We were born in sin because we are descendants of Adam and Eve. Therefore, that sin debt is owed by every human born on the earth. The only way you can avoid paying that debt is by choosing to reconnect to the Father through Jesus.

Often, when people hear the message of Jesus, they think one of two things:

1. Jesus died on the cross for their sins, so they can live and do whatever they want OR
2. Jesus died on the cross for their sins, so they must spend their lives on the Earth trying to repay Him for the sacrifice He made.

Choice two is called "salvation by works." The problem with both thought patterns is that they focus on the "I" component, not God's love, which is the only thing that makes our redemption possible.

If you are new to the story of Jesus, I think now would be a great time to read it. The story of Mary, the virgin mother of Jesus, Joseph, Mary's fiancé, and the birth of Jesus can be found in Matthew Chapters 1-2 and Luke Chapters 1-2. It is an amazing narrative that reveals that Jesus was conceived by the Holy Spirit. The Holy Spirit placed Jesus in the womb of Mary. Jesus grew up with temptations like every other human, but He never sinned. A sinless life was necessary for Him to be the sacrificial Lamb of God. He was the spotless Lamb whose life paid the debt owed by humanity. The Bible assures us of this promise in John 3:16, "*For God so loved the world that He gave His only begotten Son, that whoever believes in Him should not perish but have everlasting life.*" God is just and righteous; therefore, forgiveness and reconciliation required a perfect sacrifice, one born of flesh but without sin. That sacrifice was the person of Jesus.

Let's take a closer look at the two viewpoints people usually take concerning salvation:

Jesus paid the price, so I can do what I want

First, we must remember that our sins are the very reason Jesus came to die. God does not take sin lightly. In fact, He has a plan to judge it. Paul warns us:

But in accordance with your hardness and your impenitent heart you are treasuring up for yourself wrath in the day of wrath and revelation of the righteous judgment of God, who "will render to each one according to his deeds "eternal life to those who by patient continuance in doing good seek for glory, honor, and immortality; but to those who are self-seeking and do not obey the truth, but obey unrighteousness—indignation and wrath, tribulation and anguish, on every soul of man who does evil, of the Jew first and also of the Greek; but glory, honor, and peace to everyone who works what is good, to the Jew first and also to the

Greek. For there is no partiality with God. (Romans 2:5-11)

These verses explicitly show that God will judge sin.

Jesus' sacrifice covers our sins, so we have the ability to be transformed into God's original design. When we accept Jesus, we agree we can never pay for our sins. He alone meets the criteria required by God, which is to live a sinless life that glorifies God. Since sin is repulsive to God and payment came at a very heavy price, it should be no surprise that continuing in a life of sin, which is supported by Satan, is not acceptable. The Bible speaks about this in Act 3:19, *"Repent ye therefore, and be converted, that your sins may be blotted out, when the times of refreshing shall come from the presence of the Lord."* Our part is to repent and **turn away from** sin; we are not to indulge in it.

Jesus paid up front. I must repay Him with my works.

The second error concerning salvation is the false belief that since Jesus paid up front, we must pay Him back with our works. This is also not true. "For *by grace you have been saved through faith, and that not of yourselves; it is the gift of God, not of works, lest anyone should boast*" (Ephesians 2:8-9). We see that God was not looking for a repayment; He was just restoring order to what He originally created. Humans could never repay Him with the works of our sinful flesh. Sanctification comes as we rely on Holy Spirit to help us live the life God created for us. If we could achieve our salvation with works, some people would boast about what they are doing and elevate themselves over others. The Bible is very clear that we are all equal in the eyes of our Lord and Creator. No one is more important than the other. Peter said, *"Of a truth I perceive that God is no respecter of persons"* letting us know that God loves all His children the same"

(Acts 10:34).

God loves you no matter what you have done. He has made a way for you to be fully restored to Him through the sacrifice He made by the blood of Jesus. Jesus is the only one who could and has satisfied the requirement of being a sinless sacrifice. He is the only way to be restored to a right relationship with God. All you have to do is accept Him and allow His life to pay the price for your sins. If you have never accepted Jesus as your Saviour, now is a great time to pause for a moment and listen to God's voice. He is always calling out to His children to bring them home to Him. Sit quietly for a moment and listen. *"If we confess our sins, He is faithful and just to forgive us our sins, and to cleanse us from all unrighteousness"* (1 John 1:9). This may the time you will encounter Him. I don't want you to miss it. If you hear Him speak, engage Him today by saying this simple prayer,

God, I am a sinner, but now, I understand I need a Savior who is Jesus. I open my heart to Him and ask Him to come and live inside me. I ask Him to shape my life to look and live as He did. Come into my heart and save me.

If you just had your first encounter with Jesus, welcome to the family. If you had a previous encounter, thank Jesus for a renewed commitment to be more on fire for God than ever before.

Chapter Four

Adoption – Our Identity in Christ

After I was saved, I was not sure what my life was going to be like. I had grown up in church, so I thought I knew all the external things necessary to be in good standing with God. I assumed I could just mimic whatever I saw the people at church do. Based on my observations, I was supposed to go to church, read my Bible, tithe, be a good person, and do good things. That is, of course, what religion tells us is Christian behavior. I needed to do something to prove to the world I was worthy to be a Christian, right? No, that is not the case.

What many people do not understand is that being a Christian and a follower of Jesus is not about us proving to the world we are Christians. Being a disciple of Jesus is actually about what Jesus did in our hearts by transforming us from the inside out. When we are born again, we are adopted into God's family. As we develop in our relationship with Him, the spirit of Christ shines through us.

In the early days following my salvation, I started doing what most people do. I started "working" on looking like a Christian. Don't get me wrong; the Holy Spirit did remove some of the struggles that had held me captive; the main one being homosexuality. However, I still had emotional issues such as rejection, pride, fear, and bondage. I thought that going to church and being around other Christians would take care of that, but it didn't. I enjoyed singing and giving my tithes, even attending Wednesday night service and other church functions. All those activities made me feel as if I was really being a good Christian, but none of those things removed the feelings of rejection and inadequacy logged deep within my soul.

I continued to do Christian activities, but the condition of my soul wasn't changing. I had a routine of church activities, and I even spoke "Christianese," but something deep inside me wasn't convinced. The deep parts of my soul and personality remained unchanged. I still had emotional scars from being rejected by my biological father. I was in bondage to alcohol and food. I was a people's pleasure and fixer. I never knew how to set boundaries. What was I supposed to do with these issues? Somehow, salvation hadn't made my life perfect. What would I do now? I was going to church, sometimes reading my Bible and praying every day and night. I mimicked everything other Christians did and said we are to do. Yet, I felt in my gut something was still missing.

I didn't feel total peace in my life. I was still a people pleaser, and I tried to fix everyone else's problems. Worse still, I found myself being upset if people didn't take my advice. I wanted to gain control of the other things going on in my life that I thought would have been resolved by accepting Jesus.

Soon, I learned that accepting Christ is only the first step in the process. Salvation opens the door to be reconciled to the Father, but there is more work to be done. No one told me this in the beginning. Perhaps they didn't know it to even share it. I will share it with you now. If you don't have peace in your life and things are not going well, the good news is you have help. When you accept Jesus as your Savior, you are adopted into the family of God (Yahweh) at the same time. You are covered in the righteousness of Jesus. You are no longer a slave; you become a son or daughter of God. You have access to Holy Spirit. He comes to live inside of you and helps you become who God intended you to be when you were created. Holy Spirit teaches you how to look, think, and act like Jesus.

We were created to glorify God. Satan's goal was and still is to abort our purpose, capture our souls, and have us spend eternity in Hell with him. He doesn't want God to get glory from any portion of our lives on the earth. Even if he cannot capture our eternal souls, he still wants to inflict pain on us and God by keeping us in bondage. He tries to block us from living the abundant life we were created for. The best way for him to do that is to block the discovery of our true identity.

It is the same deception he used in the garden of Eden. He convinced Adam and Eve they needed something outside of God to be like Him. However, as the only ones created in His image, they were already like God.

In Jesus, we are no longer slaves to this world. We are adopted sons of God. This has been a huge revelation for me. In Ephesians 1:5, we are reminded that, "*He predestined us to adoption as sons through Jesus Christ to Himself, according to the kind intention of His will,*" and in Romans 8:15, "*For you have not received a spirit of slavery leading to fear again, but you have received a spirit of adoption as sons by which we cry out, "Abba! Father!"* Romans 8:16 tells us, *"The Spirit Himself testifies with our spirit that we are children of God."* There are many more Scriptures, but hopefully, you have a solid foundation now to understand how God sees you. Still, you may be perplexed about what this all actually means for your day-to-day life. It means your identity is no longer the mistakes of your past. You are a new creation—a joint heir to heaven with Jesus.

The Bible confirms in Galatians 3:29, *"And if you belong to Christ, then you are Abraham's descendants, heirs according to promise."* The word "heir" is the key to this Scripture, so I want to make sure you have a clear definition. "Heir" as defined in *Merriam-Webster's Dictionary* means:

1. One who receives **property** from an ancestor
2. One who inherits or is entitled to succeed to a hereditary **rank**, **title**, or **office;** heir to the throne.
3. One who receives or is entitled to receive something other than property from a **parent**.

Much more was happening when you accepted Jesus as your Savior than you may have ever been told. Not only is your eternity secure in Him, but you have also been adopted into the family of God. With this adoption comes the ability to live out your purpose as you were originally created in heaven. Once you ask Holy Spirit to come inside of you, He enters to assist you with your transformation. You are no longer a slave to the sins of the world. You can overcome them by relying on the same power that raised Jesus from the dead—Holy Spirit power! Your past is not what defines you. Rather, it is understanding who God created you. Salvation in Jesus won you the right to discover your true identity as a son of God.

Chapter Five

Our Relationship with Christ

I pray that you now have a firm grasp on who you are to God. You are not a slave. Accepting Jesus as your Savior makes you a son or daughter of the King. The King adopted you, so you can be in relationship with Him. Yes, I said relationship. From the beginning, God created humans to have relationship with Him, to be a part of His family. Adam and Eve were birthed from Him when He breathed the breath of life into them. He does the same thing for us today. The first breath a child takes when he is born is the breath of life being sent from God. His intention is for us to be in constant relationship with Him, with no separation. Even though we are born into sin, God has made provision through Jesus for us to have a relationship with Him.

As with any relationship, the only way you can get to know each other is by spending time together. Any strong relationship is built on a foundation of solid communication and trust. God has provided many ways for us to understand Him, including reading the Scriptures and communicating with Him through prayer.

I think most people are aware of the need to read the Bible and pray, but did you know there is a dimension of prayer that has a supernatural impact on your relationship with God and your day to day life? It comes with the second step in the process of being a follower of Christ, which is being filled with the Holy Spirit. Once you are filled with the Holy Spirit, you are given gifts from the Spirit.

Before we talk about the gifts and how to receive them, let's look at the life of Jesus and the Holy Spirit in His own life. He was the Son of God in human form, but He left His deity behind and relied on Holy Spirit, the third Person in the Trinity to perform miracles to defeat Satan.

When all the people were baptized, it came to pass that Jesus also was baptized; and while He prayed, the heaven was opened. And the Holy Spirit descended in bodily form like a dove upon Him, and a voice came from heaven which said, "You are My beloved Son; in You I am well pleased." Luke 3:21-22

Following the baptism, Jesus was led into the wilderness by Holy Spirit to be tempted by Satan. For forty days, the Devil tried to trick Jesus into sinning against God. He even used the same temptation he tricked Adam and Eve with. He tried tempting Jesus to satisfy His appetite outside of God's will. *"Then Jesus, being filled with the Holy Spirit, returned from the Jordan and was led by the Spirit into the wilderness, being tempted for forty days by the devil. And in those days, He ate nothing, and afterward, when they had ended, He was hungry"* (Luke 4:1-2, 31-37). Jesus could only resist the temptation of the Devil because He had the power of Holy Spirit.

Jesus left the garden with renewed strength. He began to teach in the synagogues and the surrounding areas. Upon

His arrival in His hometown Nazareth, He began to preach and read from the Scriptures.

And He was handed the book of the prophet Isaiah. And when He had opened the book, He found the place where it was written: The Spirit of the LORD is upon Me, because He has anointed Me to preach the gospel to the poor; He has sent Me to heal the brokenhearted, to proclaim liberty to the captives and recovery of sight to the blind, to set at liberty those who are oppressed; to proclaim the acceptable year of the LORD. (Luke 4:17-19)

Even though Jesus was sharing the truth, what He was explaining was not received by the Jewish people. *"And they said, 'Is this not Joseph's son?'"* Luke 4:22. We see that although the Savior of the world was standing before them, they were blinded to the truth. Jesus realized this was not going to change quickly, so He headed to another city, Capernaum, to preach.

Then He went down to Capernaum, a city of Galilee, and was teaching them on the Sabbaths. And they were astonished at His teaching, for His word was with authority. Now in the synagogue there was a man who had a spirit of an unclean demon. And he cried out with a loud voice, saying, "Let us alone! What have we to do with You, Jesus of Nazareth? Did You come to destroy us? I know who You are—the Holy One of God! Luke 4:31-34

Even the demons knew who they were encountering. There, in the flesh, was the Son of God standing before them. The story continues:

But Jesus rebuked him, saying, "Be quiet, and come out of him!" And when the demon had thrown him in their midst, it came out of him and did not hurt him. Then they were all amazed and spoke among themselves, saying, "What a word this is! For with authority and power He commands the unclean spirits, and they come out." And the report about Him went out into every place in the surrounding region. (Luke 4:35-36)

Demons do not respond to humans. They only respond to the voice, Word, and presence of God Almighty. When we accept Jesus and are filled with Holy Spirit, we are given the same authority Jesus used to cast out the demons on his way to Capernaum.

In addition to having authority over demons, believers are also equipped with the gifts of the Spirit. In 1 Corinthians 12:7-11, we are introduced to the gift of speaking in other tongues commonly called "speaking in tongues" or "using a prayer language." Our spirits can communicate with God directly using the heavenly language God gives to each of us. Being able to use your prayer language is very important. It provides a direct line of communication with God, spirit to spirit, without Satan being aware of what is being said. Satan cannot understand your prayer language, so you basically have a static-free, secure line to heaven.

Another gift of the Spirit is the interpretation of tongues. This supernatural gift allows someone to interpret the heavenly language in the native tongue. Think about traveling to a foreign country. An interpreter can translate the foreign language for you to understand and help you communicate. This is very similar to what happens with Holy Spirit. He interprets what God says in the language we speak on the earth.

Chapter Six

Walking in Your Authority

I pray that the picture of what Jesus did for us is taking shape in your heart and mind. However, He does not want it to stay there. He wants you to manifest your relationship with Him in your daily life. He wants you to walk in your authority as a citizen of the kingdom of heaven. One of the many things I learned in the past three years before writing this book is that I was not walking in my authority as a son of God. I believed I was responsible for how things were going in my life. This was mainly because I felt I needed to show the world that I had changed, and I wanted God to be proud of His decision to save me. I wanted to prove to Him that He made a good choice.

However, I have discovered that being a follower of Christ is more about a state of being than acting out a part. Do not get me wrong; there is a standard of living that should be demonstrated. In Galatians 5:22-23, the Bible tells us, *"But the fruit of the Spirit is love, joy, peace, longsuffering, kindness, goodness, faithfulness, gentleness, self-control.*

Against such there is no law." Still, these are fruits that develop over time. You can't force them by your will. Like a fruit tree on the earth, it takes time to produce after being planted in fertile soil. As we submit our wills to Holy Spirit and spend time in the Word of God, the fruit grows.

Now that you have a better understanding, you should rely on Holy Spirit to transform you from the inside instead of relying on your intellect and skills to make decisions. I also pray that you understand that your responsibility is simply to execute the plan God already created. The easiest and best way to understand a plan is to talk to the person who created it and get the instructions on what steps to take.

Some in society suggest we can take seven steps to be a better version of ourselves. Some encourage us to use poses of our bodies to enhance our relationship with God. Honestly, the goal isn't really about getting closer to ourselves. Self-awareness is paramount, but ultimately, your wholeness is determined by your relationship with God.

The best step to a better you is to reach out to the One who created you and ask Him directly. Read the Scriptures and spend time in His presence while using your prayer language.

I use my prayer language several times during the day. Ephesians 6:18 tells us, *"Praying always with all prayer and supplication in the Spirit, being watchful to this end with all perseverance and supplication for all the saints."* It is not a gift you take out on special occasions; it is one to use for everything.

To show you just how connected Holy Spirit is to every part of our lives, let me share a quick story. One evening, I was at a concert with my sister and the parking situation was out of control. Everyone was trying to beat each other out to their cars. I am saved, but I still don't like spending hours in a parking garage trying to exit.

As we got into the car and began to drive out, we saw two options—left or right. After a quick consult with Holy Spirit, He said, "Turn right," so we did. We soon discovered going right led us to a back exit which helped us avoid the 30-45-minute wait. No one pointed this out to us; there were no signs saying quick exit. It was Holy Spirit. This experience shows that God is interested in every aspect of our lives. We just need to stop long enough to talk to Him and get guidance.

I have also had breakthroughs in other areas of my life after understanding I am a son and adopted into the family of God. Some of the key breakthroughs I have experienced are freedom from the bondage to alcohol and the need for the approval of others. Being afraid of what people think of me is still something I struggle with, but it's much better than 10 years ago. Anything other than Holy Spirit being in control of you is not a good thing and has to be dealt with. Bondage is a demonic spirit, but it is not more powerful that Jesus. Once I understood the power that was afforded to me through my relationship with God, I got the strategy for getting a breakthrough. Slowly, I have been able to break the spirit of bondage that caused the addiction to alcohol in my life. This revelation has brought me many benefits, from reduced credit card bills to weight loss and other health gains.

My purpose in sharing this is to encourage you to start building a relationship with God, Jesus, and Holy Spirit now. They are waiting to help you achieve victory in every area of your life while you are physically here on the earth and after.

Chapter Seven

He Chose Me

I have always been a driven person but that drive to push ahead caused me to lose sight of what was important. My focus became my possessions—house, car, watches, money—everything but God. It was all about me, myself, and I. Even when I was doing things for other people, I wanted to make sure it was advertised so I could be seen as the generous one. I wanted people to like me and desire to be around me.

After careful examination and some great Holy Spirit field counselors, I have learned the driving force for my people pleasing was the fear coming from the spirit of rejection. Somewhere deep inside, I feared that being me was not enough. It drove me to give money that I didn't really have to give and to buy things on credit I really couldn't afford to purchase. I did these things all because I wanted praise from people. Even if I had to do a little extra, I was willing to in order to make sure I didn't have face rejection. Their presence made me feel wanted and needed.

It may sound really sad that I felt this way about myself, but it's true. However, by the grace of God through Jesus, I now know the truth. Not only did Jesus die to save my soul, He also died to allow me to be in relationship with Him, Holy Spirit, and God the Father. I now understand true acceptance and love that can free me from any bondage or rejection. I was covering up my fears with people-pleasing and over generosity.

Don't get me wrong. God built me to be a generous person, but Satan used it to make me extend myself in areas that were not my responsibility. Once I understood my identity, I discovered that Satan tried to get me to be out of balance with my giving. That's one of his primary tools. He often takes things that aren't inherently bad and gets us to misuse them or take them out of balance. That's the very reason we must depend on Holy Spirit to instruct us.

Now that I am better connected to my true identity in Christ, I have a desire to help others like you connect to your true identity. God looked past all my mess, as well as the mistakes and sins I committed against Him. He offered me a choice to become one with Him through Jesus. Because I said, "yes," He uses me to my highest potential as a soldier in His army. I never have to worry about losing my relationship with Him or working to keep it because at the end of it all. . .

HE CHOSE ME!

Conclusion

(The Great Commission)

I pray you have learned something from the pages of this book that will guide you into a deeper relationship with God the Father, God the Son, and God the Holy Spirit.

We are all sinners and fall short of the glory of God. We were born in sin and condemned to live eternally separated from God in the pit of Hell. However, Scripture reveals that God has provided a way back to Him. That way has a name: Jesus.

I feel impressed to remind you that we are in a very real war between good and evil. The final chapters in the book of Revelation show us that Christ is victorious, so it would only make sense to become a part of the winning team. When we become soldiers in the army of God, it is our duty to carry out the Great Commission and share the gospel of Jesus Christ.

God gave everything to restore us to our original glory. If you have not accepted Jesus, don't wait. Do it today. He didn't just choose me. He Chose You Too!

www.ingramcontent.com/pod-product-compliance
Lightning Source LLC
LaVergne TN
LVHW091321080426
835510LV00007B/595